A Better Mule

by Tom Sato
illustrated by Rusty Fletcher

Core Decodable 69

Bothell, WA • Chicago, IL • Columbus, OH • New York, NY

MHEonline.com

Copyright © 2015 McGraw-Hill Education

All rights reserved. No part of this publication may be reproduced or distributed in any form or by any means, or stored in a database or retrieval system, without the prior written consent of McGraw-Hill Education, including, but not limited to, network storage or transmission, or broadcast for distance learning.

Send all inquiries to:
McGraw-Hill Education
8787 Orion Place
Columbus, OH 43240

ISBN: 978-0-02-143353-7
MHID: 0-02-143353-4

Printed in the United States of America.

2 3 4 5 6 7 8 9 DOC 20 19 18 17 16 15

This is Doctor Hugo.
And this is Rose, a pupil.

They make robots.
They made a robot mule.
What for?

A live mule is cute.

Will it do what humans tell it?

"Go!"

Nope! A live mule will not go!
It is stubborn.

This is Doctor Hugo's mule.
It is not cute.

Is this robot mule stubborn?
Will it do what humans tell it?

We will have a test.
Rose will talk to the robot mule.

"Go! Go!"

There is a problem.

The mule will not go.

Doctor Hugo is checking the fuel.
Is fuel the problem?

Fuel is not the problem.

Is it a fuse?

Rose opens the unit.

A fuse is not the problem.
Is this robot unit broken?

Doctor Hugo and Rose check it.
The robot unit is not broken.

What is the problem?
Doctor Hugo will tell us.

"A live mule is stubborn."

"A robot mule is also stubborn."